GHOSTS
AND
GRAVESTONES sm
IN
ST. AUGUSTINE
FLORIDA

GHOSTS
AND
GRAVESTONES _{sm}
IN
ST. AUGUSTINE
FLORIDA

JOHN F. STAVELY

Historic Tours of America, Inc.
St. Augustine, Florida

© Copyright 2005

Historic Tours of America, Inc.

201 Front Street, Suite 224, Key West, FL 33040

All rights reserved

Library of Congress Control Number 2004105969

ISBN Number: 0-9752698-1-X

Second Edition 2015

Author – John F. Stavely

General Editor – Dana Ste. Claire

Publication Design & Production-SGS Design, New Smyrna Beach, FL

2nd printing by Key West Publishing, LLC

Photographs courtesy – John F. Stavely

Historic Photographs courtesy – Karen Harvey

Cover Art: A messenger of an ancient soul.

Key West
PUBLISHING, LLC

ACKNOWLEDGMENTS

Listing all of the people who contributed to this book would be impossible. Many thanks to everyone who was involved and special thanks to Historic Tours of America, Chris Belland and Ed Swift III for developing the creative environment needed to produce this book.

Without the support of the following people this book would not exist:

All the great people led by Ed Swift IV at Old Town Trolley Tours of St. Augustine and Ghosts & Gravestones.

All the great people at Ghost tours of St. Augustine

The St. Augustine Historical Society

The Augustine Paranormal Society

Diane Lane and the great people at Ancient City Ghost Tours

Bob Wentzslaff

Harry Stafford

Dana Ste. Claire

Kate, Jesse, John, Aaron, and Ben

Everyone Else (you know who you are!)

Special thanks to Karen Harvey for her advice and photographs.

Most of all, endless thanks goes to my wonderful wife, Cindy, who listens to my late night ramblings with great interest, and to my family who smiles and nods politely when I talk about the paranormal. Lastly, to Carly the Magnificent, who inspires me to live large and be my most creative each day. She always makes me smile…

"Never fear shadows.
They simply mean that there's a light somewhere nearby"

— Ruth E. Renkei

A gathering of three

CONTENTS

Winged sentries of another world.

INTRODUCTION

My belief in the supernatural took a convincing turn in 1993. The events that happened over several weeks in Maryland would forever change the way I thought about paranormal experiences and would convince me that something was happening beyond any understanding.

It began simply enough. My two bedroom home was in the middle of a newer neighborhood about 45 minutes south of Washington D.C. Most of the houses there were five or six years old and filled with young families like mine. I never noticed anything unusual about the house until the events began.

I arrived home from work one evening and went to change clothes in the bedroom. Sitting upright in the middle of the floor was a blue vase that normally rested on the chest of drawers against the wall. What caught my attention was how far away from the wall it was and that it looked as if it was intentionally placed there. I picked it up and returned it to the front of the mirror where it belonged. After dinner and some television, I walked down the hallway to the bedroom and stopped dead in my tracks. The vase was sitting upright in the middle of the room again, but now it was also surrounded by a matte frame that had been attached to the mirror next to it on the wall. My heart began to race as I wondered how the vase and frame could have gotten there almost ten feet away. All of us had been in the living room the whole evening. Was someone playing a joke? My sons were two and four years old at the time and could not have removed them. My wife reacted as I had and we tried to recreate the events, but we could not. No matter how we tipped the vase or dropped the matte, we could not get the vase and frame to end up where they were in the middle of the room. It just didn't make sense. What was going on?

Three nights later, I was sitting in the living room with my family when we heard a "thump" from the kitchen. When we investigated, nothing seemed out of place until we noticed a small vase sitting in the middle of the kitchen table. The small, rose colored vase had belonged to my wife's grandmother and sat on a high shelf almost four feet away. Did it fall almost six feet? Why didn't it break or roll off the table? The vase was returned to the shelf only to reappear on the table two hours later!

As I stood in the kitchen the next day, I heard another "thump" from the hallway and I ran out to see what caused it. Somehow, the globe from the bathroom ceiling light was sitting on the floor of the hallway. This meant that the glass cover had to fall from the ceiling to the linoleum bathroom floor

1

without breaking and then travel another eight feet to the middle of a carpeted hallway. Now I was starting to panic.

Things were quiet for several days as the objects stopped moving, but I was becoming increasingly agitated and restless. Something did not feel right and I simply could not explain away the events as natural occurrences. I was wary of telling anyone about what had happened and tried to forget the strange events. Then the ghost began to appear.

For many nights, I kept waking up around 3 a.m. I had a lingering feeling that something was wrong and would double check the doors and look in on the sleeping boys to make sure. All seemed in order until the fourth night. As I sat up in bed once again at three in the morning, I saw something

Strange light at sunset.

2

move in my room and I turned towards the door of the bedroom to see an eerie, foggy figure hovering. It was thicker than smoke, almost two feet high, and oval in shape. I stared for almost a minute trying to decide if I was still asleep when it suddenly faded away. The next night it was back, only larger, and this ectoplasm floated there as if watching me, then faded away. Two more nights passed until I saw it again in the same spot. Now it was almost five feet high and touched the ground and began to take on the shape of a person. I could not decide if it was a man or woman. Whatever it was, I was not brave enough to get any closer to find out. Then it moved. Not towards me, but out the door and toward the bedroom my sons shared. Now with all my will and fighting past my fear I shook my wife, who oddly would not wake up, and I ran to my sons room not knowing what I would find. My sons were sleeping soundly in their beds. The apparition had disappeared.

The next morning over breakfast, my four-year-old son suddenly announced; *"Daddy, last night there was a man in my room."* A chill went up my spine as I suggested to him that I had been in his room last night and it must have been me he saw. *"Oh no,"* he said, *"the man I saw wasn't you. He had a long beard and was dressed in blue. I didn't see you Daddy."* Fear swept over me and I began to shake. Did my son dream this or was a presence visiting us in our home? Were we in danger? My mind was reeling.

Three nights later the events came to an end. I awoke around 3:30 a.m. and saw the presence standing at the doorway. I stood up and the apparition floated out of the door and down the hallway toward our living room. My heart was racing as I started to follow it. Looking down the hallway, I saw nothing. I slowly walked past the bathroom and looked in to see a glowing swirl of thick fog. Before I could react, it rushed towards me and crashed into me as I tried to retreat to the wall. It felt like a bucket of cold water was thrown on me as this apparition passed through me. The strange events stopped after that night. We moved out not long after.

To this day, I do not know what the entity was or why it was there. We did find out that even though the house was new, the land under it had a long history. After the assassination of President Lincoln, the soldiers tracking John Wilkes Booth had camped there and later arrested Dr. Mudd who lived only a few miles away. Could this explain the man in blue my son saw in his bedroom? I do not know. What I do know is that the events I experienced opened my mind to the endless paranormal possibilities that exist.

Twilight Silhouette

"Alice laughed. "There's no use trying" she said. "One can't believe impossible things." "I daresay you haven't had much practice," said the Queen. "When I was your age, I always did it half an hour a day. Why, sometimes, I've believed as many as six impossible things before breakfast."

— Lewis Carol

Do You Believe?

"The most beautiful thing we can experience is the mysterious. It is the source of all true art and science. He to whom this emotion is a stranger, who can no longer pause to wonder and stand rapt in awe, is as good as dead, his eyes are closed."
— Albert Einstein

Do you believe in ghosts? Have you ever wondered what exists beyond our normal senses of sight, smell, touch, taste, and hearing? Are you curious? Journey with us on a fascinating exploration of the Ghosts and Gravestones found in St. Augustine, Florida —

The town that some consider to be the most active haunted place in the world.

Debates continue about the nature of our encounters with the paranormal and theories abound. Perhaps the best way to decide is through careful study of documented paranormal evidence followed by frequent "field study" visits to the most haunted places. St. Augustine, Florida might be the best laboratory available.

Prior to European settlement of St. Augustine in 1565, this area was inhabited for thousands of years by vast Native American kingdoms. The town we know today is built on land with a rich and engaging heritage of human emotion and drama. The lives that were lived over the centuries have accumulated their energy and left an enduring after glow in this place. Just walk down the streets and you will understand…

We can spend much of our lives insulated from the world around us. Busy with activity, we rarely take the time to stand perfectly still and quiet in the middle of a room and become aware of what might happen. Sometimes we have no choice…

This book explores strange and unusual occurrences, which took place over several hundred years, in St. Augustine Florida, but does not offer the only explanations available. In some cases, names, locations and circumstances were altered to protect the privacy of the individuals involved but in every case the accuracy of what happened and how it was experienced by those present has been preserved.

The rest is for you to decide…

YOU'LL END UP IN THE POUR HOUSE

The usual crowd was gathering at their favorite watering hole, Murphy's Pour House, to begin the weekend. The voices grew louder inside the old building when a sudden sharp popping sound split the air. The bartender jumped to one side as five bottles in the wine rack began to explode one after the other. The patrons stared transfixed as next an ashtray jumped off the shelf and crashed to the floor. Then, one by one, a row of glasses dropped to the floor from the overhead rack nearby. Each one pausing like a parachute before leaping into the air. No one spoke for several minutes as the bartender reached for the dustpan to clean up. He kept it handy because it wasn't the first time this scene had been played out with broken glass scattered everywhere. It wouldn't be the last, either.

Who lurks on the top floor?

Since it opened in 1999, Murphy's Pour House had been a pleasant place to meet with friends for good food, music and conversation but behind the scenes some of the people who worked there were frightened. Too many strange incidents had left them all puzzled and jittery. Why did the wine bottles explode and how did the glasses fall out of the rack time after time? Many attempts were made to discover the source of these episodes or recreate them with no success. They wanted answers but there were none. Finally, paranormal investigators were contacted and the bizarre incidents were documented for further investigation. It proved to be a small comfort to those who worked there as several quit including a chef that, one day, discovered his young daughter sitting at a table talking to an unseen person next to her. She was having a wonderful conversation with the air, it seemed. When he asked his daughter who she was talking to, she turned to him and very sincerely said, *"can't you see the little boy too?"* It was all the chef could take. He scooped up his daughter and resigned on the spot. Just three days before, it turns out, he was walking to the kitchen when he saw a man standing at the sink. Thinking it was a lost customer he entered the kitchen and started to speak when the figure vanished. Twice in one week was too much and he could not be convinced to return there. Since then, many reports of an unseen young boy talking with children have surfaced. Confused parents quickly relate the incidents to the wait staff, ask for their bill and leave the building.

Several people have heard murmuring, unseen voices that seem to speak an unclear word or sentence. They can never find the source of these voices. Others have been touched on the arm or leg as they sat in the dining room. Bartenders on the second floor are convinced that, when they step away, random letters appear on a chalkboard behind the bar. Candles on the tables and bars are mysteriously found burning after they have been extinguished at closing time. One night, after closing, an acorn fell on top of the owner's head as he crossed the dance floor upstairs. He stared for a long time at the acorn on the floor because he knew the ceiling above his head was solid drywall. Where had it come from?

So much activity seems to occur in this building at 72 Spanish Street that it is uncanny. Dozens of witnesses confirm a long list of odd events and strange happenings. Almost one hundred years ago, this building served as a laundry house for the Hotel Ponce de Leon built by millionaire industrialist, Henry Flagler. Are those workers still with us?

Murphy's Pour House closed its doors in 2001 and at the time of this writing the building is vacant. As far as we know…

CATALINA GOES HOME

She never left, it seems… she lingers at 46 Avenida Menendez on the Bay front of St. Augustine. The dark red building, which is now called Harry's restaurant is popular and bustling with activity. That is probably why the female apparition is seen so often because there are a lot of witnesses. Many link the apparition seen walking the hallways to a women named Catalina de Porras who grew up in this home until she was ten years old in 1763.

In October of that year the British occupation of St. Augustine forced Catalina and her family to leave for Cuba. Catalina, unable to understand why she had to leave the home she loved so much, made a vow to return one day. Twenty years later, in 1784, she got her chance. Arriving with her husband in St. Augustine, Catalina began petitioning the Governor to return to her childhood home. Five years later, the house was hers again. Now thirty-six years old, she began restoring the memories of her childhood in the house. Her dreams were

fulfilled. She was home again at last. But fate was cruel. Six short years later, Catalina breathed her last breath on this earth.

But some say she never left. The staff at Harry's relate stories of a woman's reflection seen in mirrors as well as many odd encounters with a woman in old-fashioned clothing who is seen throughout the building. Sometimes it's just a glimpse of her down the hallway or in an empty room but occasionally there is more. One customer ran out of the second floor restroom after feeling a presence in the room. She felt as though an unseen person was watching her, and the feeling was just too real.

Is Catalina there?

Unable to shake the notion that she was not alone in the restroom, the woman retreated downstairs. She said, *"I just had to get out of there."* Many people report a similar feeling of being "followed." This fully formed apparition is often encountered walking past people in hallways or standing in a room before vanishing into thin air.

Spontaneous fires ignite in the fireplace and snuffed candles re-light when no one is near them. Objects appear to move from one place to another and the strong smell of perfume fills the air at times. Passers by report seeing odd figures of both men and women looking out of the building and photographs have revealed images in the windows.

Apparitions are often seen in the windows at Harry's Restaurant on Avenida Menendez.

Maybe Catalina is still there. If so, she may have been joined by a male apparition. A male apparition who is thought to be connected with a man who died in the home. A tall, dark figure dressed in clothes from the late eighteen hundreds is seen by employees and customers of the restaurant. He typically walks down the staircase, through the dining room and then vanishes. Who is this mystery man? We may never know. What we do know is that the dark red building on the bay front is making believers out of lots of folks who never did.

WHO GOES THERE?

The DeMesa House, in the City's Spanish Quarter Museum, is open for guided public tours on the hour. The history is fascinating as you step back in time, but what makes this attraction most noteworthy is the unusual phenomenon that occur there on a regular basis. Visitors have reported cold spots and the sensation that some unseen person is in the room with them. Floors creak when no one is there and footsteps can be heard when the house is empty. On one occasion, a man who works in the house as a tour guide, was reading in a upstairs hallway when he heard footsteps coming up the stairs. Knowing the door was locked the man expected the visitor to turn around and go back down the steps and wait until the next tour started. The footsteps didn't stop. Suddenly the hollow footsteps were in the hallway coming towards him even though he could see nothing there. He stood perfectly still as they passed him and continued on. At this point he noticed a shadow on the far wall cast by the window behind him. It looked like the image of a young girl walking down the hall. As the footsteps grew fainter, he tried to understand what just happened. He had no explanation.

Apparitions of both men and women are often seen in the house. Photographs taken inside have revealed strange blurs, orbs of light, energy ribbons and streaks. At times what seems to be a face or a figure is captured on film. In some photos white light fills the whole frame. Others show misty fog in one part of the room. Is this house occupied by unseen others? Do they make their presence known from time to time? You are invited to discover for yourself the inexplicable activities in this Historic house. Just be sure to bring your camera along…

The DeMesa House in the Spanish Quarter on St. George Street hosts tourists, present and seemingly past.

10

PIRATES, SOLDIERS AND SAILING SHIPS

"Beyond the ken of mortal men, beneath the wind and waves.
There lies a land of shells and sand, of chasms, crags and caves,
Where coral castles climb and soar, where swaying seaweeds grow,
And all around without a sound the ocean currents flow"

— The Sign of the Seahorse by Graeme Base

In the long history of seafaring, St. Augustine stood as an important port of call for trade and treachery. From the beginning, pirates chased the treasure laden Spanish Galleons up the coast and powerful monarchies laid siege to the town. The Atlantic Ocean beckons visitors to remember the sailing ships of the past that were once the lifeblood of this town.

The Atlantic Ocean just beyond the sand dunes holds the remains of countless shipwrecks and lost souls.

11

THE LITTLE FORGOTTEN PLACE

In Europe long ago, castles and mansions often had hidden somewhere in the structure "a little forgotten place." A secret room that served as a dungeon for the hosts to rid themselves of enemies or people they disliked. These carefully concealed rooms were perfect for making people suddenly disappear. But perhaps this European custom came to St. Augustine one gray, dreary day long ago...

Sergeant Tuttle and his men pushed with all their might but the old Spanish cannon did not budge. They tried once more and stopped. Ever since Sergeant Tuttle had been assigned to St. Augustine's Fort Marion on the bay front he had tried to keep things orderly. Now in 1838, he and his men were attempting, with great difficulty, to move the aging brass and iron cannons around on the upper gun deck. As they pushed once more a cracking sound panicked the men. They all jumped back just in time to see the floor collapse and the huge brass canon drop through the hole! No one was hurt but the men were now faced with retrieving the lost cannon from the room below. Several men went down the worn stone steps and looked in the last room under the gun deck. It was empty. Quickly looking in surrounding rooms they were astonished to find them empty too. Where was the cannon? They marched back up to the top and looked again through the hole. There was the cannon at the bottom. They discovered that the cannon had fallen into a room that was now sealed. The soldiers grabbed sledgehammers and headed for the last room in the corner.

Still standing guard.

12

A "little forgotten place" underneath the tower.

Pounding on the crumbling coquina shell stone, the men soon broke through the wall to discover another room sealed from view. As they peered through the opening, a burst of sweet smelling air washed over them. It smelled like a thousand roses. The men looked at one another uneasily before venturing inside. They found the cannon in the hidden room and soon returned it by ropes to the upper gun deck of the fort but as they labored to move it out of the room they stumbled upon… bones… many shapes and sizes of bones.

What was this place and why had it been sealed? Who was responsible for it's construction?

Searching for clues, local historians have discovered a possible connection. Garrison Commandant Garcia Marti was commander of the Fort in 1784. During this time his wife and his first officer were suspected of having a secret affair. Soon they both disappeared and were never heard from again. Did they run off together to start a new life in some distant land or had they been caught, imprisoned in a "little forgotten place" to wither away. Did a curious accident in 1838 reveal their final resting place?

The defensive fort known today as the Castillo de San Marcos was named Fort Marion in 1821 when the United States took over possession of Florida. Construction began in 1672 and finished 23 years later so the knowledge of its construction history is shrouded by time. What did Sergeant Tuttle really discover?

13

FIRE AND STEEL

St. Augustine was founded in 1565 and a fierce conflict followed. Ships of the French fleet descended from the north and attacked the newly arrived Spanish forces led by Don Pedro Menéndez de Avilés. The French soldiers were confident that they could easily overwhelm the Spanish troops until suddenly, without warning, the French forces were pummeled by a furious storm that erupted off the coast and smashed their ships. Less than two hundred soldiers managed to struggle into the harbor and were soon captured by the Spanish just south of town near Matanzas Inlet. The Spanish had no food or housing for the French prisoners so they gave them a choice: become one of us or die. The French refused to convert to Spanish ways. One by one, they were slaughtered by sword and thrown into the bay until the waters ran bright red for three days...

Touching the heavens.

The bay is mysterious and ever changing. Some believe that the Spirits of those victims of the past remain in the waters of Mantanzas Bay and manifest themselves on certain nights. There are many reports of the water transforming itself into a bright red hue on moonlit nights. At other times, boaters looking over the sides of their vessels are shocked to see lifeless eyes staring back at them from the water below. They appear for only an instant and then are gone.

Frozen in time.

One sailor experienced the sight of an eerie green glow deep under the water that began rising up towards him. Frightened, he sped away in his boat. Another woman swore she saw the apparitions of Spanish soldiers on the sandy shore waving for her to come closer.

She did not and they vanished when she turned back to look again. Some even claim to have seen ships from the past sailing into the harbor at night. Glowing in the moonlight, these vessels at first appear to be historical reenactments until they slowly fade away. Are there pirates returning to plunder again or explorers from the past looking for new lands? Or are they just imaginary visions? The frequency and detail of these sightings would suggest that something is going on beyond our understanding.

Only time will help us solve these mysteries, but if you find yourself on the haunted waters of Mantanzas Bay be careful when you look over the side of the boat... someone may be looking back...

THE SHIP OF DOOM

She sailed into the harbor in 1821, a supply ship from Havana, Cuba. Normally, a supply ship was good news for the town but not this time. When she was boarded it was discovered that not one sailor survived. All hands were lost, even the captain. This doomed ship would bring darkness upon the town as victims of yellow fever began appearing shortly after her arrival. Before it was over, hundreds would succumb to the "yellow jack." Most were quickly buried in mass graves near what is now called the Huguenot cemetery, just outside the City Gates.

Countless souls pass these gates.

Just beyond the city gates at the north end of Saint George Street lies the Huguenot Cemetery. A desperate need to bury the victims of a yellow fever epidemic that struck St. Augustine in 1821 led to its creation. The burial fee was $4.00 for persons with means to pay. Mass graves were used because the rate of fallen victims reached over a dozen a day. The church bell that traditionally rang the death toll constantly was finally ordered silenced out of respect for the sick and dying. By 1827, the fence around the graveyard was gone and the burials extended over the surrounding land. The burials were finally stopped on August 13, 1884 when citizens, concerned about the health effects of burying bodies so close to the city, closed it once and for all.

In looking back, we realize that not all the graves are accounted for inside the walls and fences that exist today. Time has changed the landscape. Over 400 bodies were buried there but only 94 markers remain. Some monuments surely fell apart over the years but where are the others buried?

Go to the Huguenot Cemetery and as you stand near the wall closest to the City Gates, look down under your feet. Chances are that you will be standing on someone's remains… someone all but forgotten. But watch carefully as you walk past this place. Some residents believe that those fever victims return as apparitions to walk the town, not realizing they have passed.

One such apparition is seen standing between the city Gates. Many believe she is Elizabeth, the young daughter of the Gatekeeper, who died of the yellow fever. She is seen waving to cars as they pass on the street. Shopkeepers are approached by new visitors asking about the historical reenactor who is greeting folks at the City Gates. They confess that no historical actor stands at those gates. Since she appears to be real, many have mistaken her for an actual person. When they look more closely however, she either disappears or begins to fade into a misty shadow of herself, becoming transparent and unreal. If you stand between those city gates you may feel a heaviness in the air followed by a cold wind. Be sure to say hello to Elizabeth if you do.

Phantom figures… can you see them?

GRANDMA WILL BE FINE

Grandma Paffe passed from this earth in 1924 and the strange events that surrounded her death are still talked about today. She lived with her grandson at 49 St. George Street in a two-story house that no longer exists. Because she was aging and spent most of her time in her room upstairs, Grandma Paffe often had visitors to the home. But on her final night, her visitors were of the paranormal kind...

The Paffes ran two successful businesses in the downstairs of the St. George Street building and the grandson was kept busy with daily responsibilities. He decided to hire a nurse to look after his grandmother and was relieved to find Maggie Hunter. She and Grandma got along very well and three nights each week, Maggie would sit with Grandma while checking her pulse and breathing. They would talk and laugh into the night until Maggie had to leave.

One night as Maggie sat on Grandma's bed the sound of wind and rain signaled a growing storm. Maggie peered out of the window and saw the rain blowing sideways down the empty streets. So powerful was the storm that Maggie was afraid to leave and asked to spend the night. The grandson readily agreed. Just after dinner, Maggie brewed a cup of tea for grandma and climbed the stairs to the second floor. As she started down the hallway to Grandma's room, she started to hear someone in the room with Grandma Paffe. Kneeling by the bed was a dark figure. Maggie grew uneasy as she stared. No one could have gotten into the house during the storm. As the figure stood from its kneeling position, Maggie realized it was a nun. The sisters would stop by from time to time to visit but tonight the storm should have stopped even the bravest soul. Maggie took a step closer and dropped the teacup from her hand when she realized that the nun was transparent and she could see right through her. Maggie turned, screamed and ran down the steps. The grandson caught her in his arms and tried to calm her, but she was too hysterical. As she quickly babbled her story of the ghostly nun, the grandson stared at her with a strange look in his eyes. When she was calm he began to explain about "the good sister." For months the apparition had been appearing at the foot of Grandma's bed, but he had not told anyone about it. Maggie slumped in her chair, not knowing what to do. She could not leave because of the storm but she did not want to stay in the house with a ghost! Try as she might, Maggie could not sleep. She paced the floors with the image of the nun clear in her mind.

The next evening the ghost nun did not appear to Maggie and she was relieved. Perhaps she had just imagined the whole thing after all. Maybe the Grandson was just trying to calm her by saying he had seen it too. Maggie walked up the stairs to Grandma's room, supper in her hand, confident she would never see the ghost again. She was wrong. Entering the room, Maggie

A glimpse of the past.

saw the image of a soldier standing at attention next to Grandma's bed. The ghostly apparition never moved as Maggie screamed and ran downstairs to find the Grandson. He grabbed her tightly as she wailed over and over that a soldier stood next to Grandma's bed upstairs. Staring deeply into her eyes, the Grandson gasped, *"Maggie, my Grandmother has died!"* He pushed Maggie away and ran up the stairs.

Maggie found him next to Grandma's bed sobbing uncontrollably. Carefully, she moved to the other side of the bed and lifted Grandma Paffe's arm to feel for a pulse. She felt nothing… She turned to the grandson and asked him, *"How did you know she was gone when I told you about the soldier?"* Between sobs he answered. *"Oh Maggie, my Grandma told me stories my whole life. One was about the day she would pass from this world. She believed that a soldier would come upon her death and escort her to another place."*

The soldier and the nun have not been seen since 1924. Whoever they were… whatever they were… the visions seemed to be connected only to Grandma Paffe. When she passed, they disappeared too.

19

UNDER THE LIGHT WE PLAY

Stand perfectly still outside the light tower of the St. Augustine Lighthouse and listen for them... the children's voices... laughing and playing. Just outside they can be heard too. Calling out to one another, giggling and hiding. Just listen...

In 1873, a terrible tragedy struck. Three young girls, ages 7, 12 and 15, lost their lives at the lighthouse when a construction railcar they and a neighbor were playing in plunged into the Atlantic Ocean. Despite valiant attempts to save them, only the neighbor girl survived the incident. Several months later the sounds of children began to drift up the scaffolds to the men laying bricks for the tower. Knowing it was unsafe for children to play below they would climb down to warn them but never found anyone there. They reluctantly related these occurrences to the construction supervisor, Hezekiah Pittee, hoping for an explanation. Pittee would sadly shake his head and offer none. Who could blame him? It was two of his daughters that perished in the awful accident and, in his grief, maybe he could not believe that they were truly gone.

Visitors and staff report seeing a young girl's apparition inside the Keeper's house, near the spiral staircase. One couple saw a teenaged girl on the lower floor that they thought worked for the museum because she was dressed in old-fashioned clothing. When they turned to ask her a question, she was gone. They asked about her in the gift shop and to their surprise were told no one was dressed in a costume that day. Many of the staff have seen a young girl looking out of a window after the building is closed. Could it be the eldest daughter who was lost in that terrible accident of 1873?

In the 1960's, a man lived in the Keeper's house and had visitors stay with him from time to time. On at least two occasions, his guests would wake up in the middle of the night to find a young girl in an antique dress standing next to the bed staring at them. They asked, *"who are you?"* The young girl smiled and disappeared...

Through the years, the children's laughter has been heard by hundreds of people. Witnesses believe that the children are happy... wherever they are...

The St Augustine Lighthouse and Museum built in the 1870's, seems to be the haunt of the ghosts of young children, and others.

THE SMOKING MAN

Visitors marvel at the beautifully renovated historic lighthouse in St. Augustine. Hours are spent looking at exhibits, climbing the tower, and reading about the lives of the Lightkeepers. From time to time, the lingering smell of cigar smoke fills your nose as you explore the property. However, searching for the source of the cigar smoke will prove futile unless you see the smoking man apparition. Pale and luminescent, he will stare at you for a moment while puffing on his cigar then turn and walk away. Do not try to follow him. Many have tried only to find themselves alone and baffled by his disappearance. He vanished along with the smell of smoke. Some believe he is a former Lightkeeper from the 1920's, Captain Rassmunsun, who remains on duty. His wife would not let him smoke in the house so he was forced to puff outside. Apparently, he is still not allowed to smoke in the house.

Former lightkeepers still roam the grounds and tower.

HOME IS WHERE YOU HANG YOUR HAT

Motto For A Front Hall

If you come cheerily,
Here shall be jest for you;
If you come wearily,
Here shall be rest for you.

If you come borrowing,
Gladly we'll loan to you;
If you come sorrowing,
Love shall be shown to you.

Under our thatch, friend,
Place shall abide for you,
Touch but the latch friend,
The door will swing wide for you!

— Nancy Byrd Turne

We feel safe within the walls of our homes and memories fill the places where we spend our time. Home can be a magnet for those seeking comfort. When we travel, the tug of home often sends us to seek out the Inn. A place that almost always was a home to someone else before us. A place where memories are strong…

HE'S LATE FOR LUNCH

Close to Le Pavillion restaurant at 47 San Marco Avenue is the Painted Lady Bed and Breakfast. Owners Will and Carey Dunnon are wonderful hosts and avid paranormal adventurers. Guests are treated to collections of gemstones, jewelry and American Indian art. One of the most interesting offerings is "Auric Photographs," designed to show the energy that surrounds the body.

The Dunnons are only the third owners of this historic house built by Charles Segui in 1910. Segui raised carrier pigeons in the home and owned a bookstore on St. George Street in town. He would ride his bicycle to and from the bookstore and always returned home for lunch so that he could feed his pigeons. It was a daily ritual for Charles Segui and one he may continue long after his passing in 1948. On several occasions the front door of the Painted Lady will burst open at mid-day with footsteps heard rushing up the staircase. Is the wind just playing tricks or does Charles return for lunch after all this time? If you see an old bicycle leaning against the porch out front, you may want to go inside and see if Charles is upstairs, quietly feeding the pigeons.

The Painted Lady beckons guests from all ages.

24

From the ashes, a resident spirit keeps watch.

THE FLAMES LEAPT HIGHER

The Castle Warden, originally built as a winter residence in 1887 by William G. Warden, a former partner of John D. Rockefeller and Henry M. Flagler, now houses Ripley's Believe It or not Museum. It served as a hotel in the early 1940's when Pulitzer Prize winning author, Majorie Kinnan Rawlings and her husband, Norton Baskin purchased it. Now it is filled with the odd and bizarre objects collected by adventurer Robert L. Ripley.

The building is a maze of corridors and hidden passages and it seems to reveal events as mystifying as the strange objects inside. Visitors recount episodes with heightened feelings of claustrophobia, sadness, joy, dread and temperature changes. One woman claims to have been held on the arm by some unseen presence. She left the building after showing hand marks on her skin to the staff.

A regular sighting is connected with a tragedy that occurred in April of 1944. Two women were staying on the upper floors when fire broke out. Although they screamed from the windows, Ruth and Betty could not be saved as they quickly succumbed to smoke inhalation.

Many report seeing a phantom woman walking through the building or looking out the upper floor windows. Often, when the staff reports to work in the morning, they notice a curtain drawn back for a few seconds and sometimes spot what appears to be a woman looking out at them. The building is locked and empty during these episodes. Could the two women still be looking for safe passage from the fire or are specters roaming these corridors? Explore this peculiar building and you may find out.

Here, the cats see what we cannot.

DO NOT WEEP FOR ME

Overlooking the bay front and just south of the Castillo de San Marco is the Casa de la Paz Inn. Restored and opened as a bed and breakfast inn in 1986, the Casa offers guests a timeless experience and some unexpected surprises. The owners are cat friendly and these delightful felines often watch something unseen crossing the room. Sometimes music boxes play with no one near them. Surprised patrons inspect the room for pranksters only to find that the music is seemingly playing on its own... or is something else responsible?

Sightings of a woman began in 1985 during construction of the Inn. A carpenter and crew were seated in the kitchen when the image of a woman dressed in black walked past them and up the steps. They were so convinced she was real that they ran up the steps after her, thinking she was a visitor in the wrong place. She could not be found in the house.

In 1986, the innkeeper, Harry, was conducting a class that involved a local author reading excerpts from his book. As Harry spoke, someone noticed a woman descend the stairs behind him carrying a suitcase and wearing vintage travel clothes. She unsuccessfully tried getting around Harry as he made his remarks and went back up the stairs. A few moments later she returned to the steps and then retreated upstairs for the last time. When Harry finished, a woman who had seen the whole thing walked up to him and declared, *"that was very rude of you."* Harry looked puzzled as she continued; *"it was rude of you not to let that woman pass by you on the stairs. Do you treat all of your guests that way?"* Harry assured her that no one had come down the stairs and furthermore, there were no guest in the building. Who had she seen? Where was this apparition going? The woman emphatically stuck to her story.

Soon after this event, guests began reporting strange events. Objects moved in their rooms, odd noises were heard and glimpses of moving figures were seen from the corner of the eye. Several guests mentioned hearing a knock on their door in the middle of the night and a female voice saying, *"Is it time to go, yet? It is time to go?"* The bravest guest would get up and peer out the door into an empty hallway, but most would just pull the covers higher and somehow try to sleep.

THEY WILL NEVER BE TOGETHER

The St. Francis Inn, founded in 1791, is the oldest in the city. Legends run deep here and you can feel the history with every step as you explore the passageways of the building. Major General William Hardee and his wife Anna owned the Inn after 1855. During this time the Major General's nephew was suspected of sharing his affections with one of the black servants and, once discovered, was ordered to stop. Knowing that their love was forbidden, the nephew took his own life on the third floor. Lily, the servant who loved him, would never be at peace again.

Major General William Hardee owned the St. Francis Inn after 1852. One of his employees still wanders the premises.

It is believed that Lily still wanders the building looking for her long, lost love. Most activity occurs in room 3 A believed to be the location of their secret meetings. Guests share tales of lights, radios, and televisions turning on and off by themselves. Women's cosmetic bags are found in the morning with scattered contents on the floor and sightings of Lily's apparition are frequent. Many have seen her carrying towels down the stairs or in the hallway and several guests have disclosed that she appeared to them in their bedrooms at night. Paranormal fans eagerly flock to this site hoping for a glimpse of Lily and a brush with the supernatural.

SHE WAITS FOR ME

A few steps from the Tolomato Catholic Cemetery on Cordova Street is the Southern Wind Inn. If you stay here or walk past, make sure you look up at the second floor balcony to see the lady in white. She is often seen standing or sitting on the balcony of this charming Inn. Guest have seen her in the hallway and on the stairs, too. Her smiling face has greeted startled guests for many years as she floats away and vanishes in the blink of an eye. No one is sure who she is but a clue to her identity might be found at the cemetery a short distance away.

The lady in white is often seen looking down from the balcony.

A woman in a white dress is sometimes seen moving back and forth near the left side of the cemetery. Could the essence, the spirit, the life force of this woman still be wandering familiar paths? Guests at the Inn sometimes experience flickering lights, odd sounds, footsteps in the hallways and sudden temperature changes of the water in the bathroom. Is she trying to communicate with us? Somewhere among the stones, vaults and wrought iron, her story may one day emerge.

Evenings are best to look for this ghostly woman who frequents the Southern Wind Inn. If you see her on the balcony wave to her... she might wave back.

IF THESE WALLS COULD TALK

Henry Morrison Flagler was already a multi-millionaire when he came on holiday to St. Augustine from New York City. The trip was long and tiring but he saw great potential in the historic town becoming a destination for winter weary northerners. Mr. Flagler was an excellent judge of potential having partnered with John D. Rockefeller and co-founding, in 1870, the Standard Oil Company. Sensing opportunity in St. Augustine, Henry Flagler improved the railroad transportation system and then built his first hotel in 1888, the Ponce de Leon. It was intended to be the grandest hotel in the country. The Rockefellers, Vanderbuilts, and five United States presidents all stayed here. Power, influence and wealth often breeds great triumph and tragedy and so too was the legacy over the years at the Hotel Ponce de Leon. Betrayal, infidelity and insanity were all guests there. Perhaps these emotional events are the source of apparitions that now appear in the building.

The Old Hotel Ponce de Leon has given way to Flagler College in modern times. Restoration is ongoing as students walk the halls, dine and sleep where the rich and famous once did a century ago. At times, the past may be intruding on the present. Students encounter a wide variety of ghostly figures in the former guest rooms, now converted to dormitories and classrooms. Many accounts tell of a young boy who plays in the hallways. He wears knee pants from a bygone era and seems to be around ten years old. Students say the sightings start when someone runs by their dorm room door and they get up and look down the hallway. Expecting to see a fellow student, they either see nothing or a young boy standing in the distance. He always looks back at them and then runs through the wall, vanishing. Sleeping coeds have woken up in the middle of the night to find the figure of a woman standing over their beds. She disappears instantly and they are left to decide if it was all just a dream.

High drama filled the halls of the hotel Ponce de Leon.

Dark skies shadowed the 1913 funeral procession of Henry Morrison Flagler outside the Ponce de Leon.

One of the most bewildering episodes involved a male student who greatly admired the man who built the original hotel, Henry Morrison Flagler. This student felt that Mr. Flagler was a wonderful entrepreneur and he hoped to follow in his footsteps when he graduated from college. Each day on his way to classes, this young man would walk by a life size statue of Henry Flagler that sits outside the front entrance to the college. Daily he would wave to the statue and say, *"How are you doing Henry? Hope to see you one day!"* What he meant was that he hoped to be like Henry Flagler one day, not that he really wanted to see him. Sometimes you must be careful what you wish for. He did not expect anything out of the ordinary as he returned to his dorm room one afternoon, closed the door and sat down at his desk to begin homework. He heard the door opening behind him and turned to see if his friends had come in without knocking, as they often did. No one was there, but the door slowly closed again. "Air pressure" must have opened and closed the door he thought to himself. As he went back to reading, the temperature began to drop and it suddenly became almost twenty degrees colder in the room. He had a strange feeling that he was not alone anymore. At that moment, a hand rested on his shoulder from behind and he jumped up from the desk frantically looking in every direction. No one was there. He raced from the room yelling as he went. His friends chased after him, finally catching up downstairs in the lobby. The young man was scared out of his wits and stammered out the events that just took place in his room. His friends were skeptical but the young man insisted and refused to return to his room. He claimed that it was haunted. The incident shook him up so much that he stayed with friends until transferring out of school a week later. He vowed never to return.

What actually took place in that room we may never fully grasp. Maybe the essence of Henry Flagler returned that day to encourage a young man with great potential and ended up scaring him away forever.

31

Ghostly music drifts down the corridors of the Alcazar.

THE DANCE GOES ON

Henry Flagler saw a need to continue building hotels in St. Augustine and the Alcazar Hotel soon appeared just across the street in 1888. Her guests attended lavish social gatherings around the world's largest indoor swimming pool, mounted "boneshakers" and tall-wheeled "ordinaries" at the bicycle academy and relaxed in Turkish baths to soothe the body. Every diversion was provided for them as laughter and conviviality rang from every floor. Such festive merrymaking can linger it seems...

In the 1980's, a restoration crew was working late one night in the old Alcazar hotel, now the Lightner Museum, when the foreman decided to send his crew home and finish the remaining work himself. After his men packed up and left he worked in silence until he heard voices in the next room. Thinking his crew has returned, he continued working and didn't pay much attention to the muffled voices in the building. Suddenly the sound of music reached his ears and he stopped to listen. The faint sound of an orchestra could be heard as he strained to listen. Now he was convinced that his men were playing a joke. He knew that none of his crew listened to orchestra music and he went to tell them to knock it off and leave him alone. But he couldn't because no one else was in the building. The foreman searched from room to room for the source of the sounds. The music and voices always drifted from one part of the building to another as his imagination started to run wild. He ran frantically from the building to look for work trucks in the parking lot but they were gone. His truck was the only one remaining. As he ran back in the building, the music and voices grew louder. Grabbing his tools, he ran from the building and vowed never to work late again. He found his crew later at a local pub where they had been for over an hour.

Others have reported similar incidents in the building. Voices, laughter, music and clinking of glasses seem to suggest that guests from the past may still be dining and dancing at the Alcazar Hotel after all these years. So raise a glass and toast the next time you walk by the hotel and listen carefully for the echoes from the past.

Guests of the Alcazar still come and go.

WE'RE BACK . . .

After 100 years, the Cordova Hotel has been restored to its original splendor as the luxurious Casa Monica Hotel. Built by Boston architect, Franklin Smith in 1888, the hotel never realized its full potential until Henry Flagler purchased it several months after its grand opening and renamed it the Cordova Hotel to compliment his Hotel Ponce de Leon and Alcazar hotels across the street. The historic property enjoyed a rebirth in 2001 when it became the Casa Monica Hotel, but some believe that more was restored there than was intended.

Franklin Smith is reported to haunt the Casa Monica Hotel building.

Reports of unusual happenings began during reconstruction as work crews started seeing apparitions throughout the building. Figures of men and women would appear briefly then disappear without a trace. Electrical devices would malfunction. Electronic door locks would lock and unlock without anyone tripping them. Drills and saws would mysteriously stop working then suddenly start for no apparent reason. Radios and televisions would turn on and off and change channels with no one near.

Once the Hotel opened the activity intensified as employees and guests shared stories of odd happenings. One man woke in the middle of the night to see a woman in a green, old-fashioned dress, standing just inside the door of his room. As he sat up, she turned and vanished through the closed door. While cleaning, the housekeeping staff sometimes discover footsteps on freshly vacuumed carpets and bedspreads as though unseen visitors are walking in the room.

An apparition that some believe to be Franklin Smith, the architect himself, has been seen inside the north corner suite peering out over the city. Guests will often ask the front desk who the man is looking out of the window. Most often he is seen from the outside but on one occasion, a maintenance worker entered the suite for repairs and was surprised to see a man standing in the living room. He apologized for the intrusion and, after the man did not respond, quickly left the room. When he checked at the front desk to find out why he had been told the room was empty when it was not, the maintenance man was shocked to learn that the room was not occupied.

Maybe Franklin Smith could never bear to leave the hotel he loved. Those who have seen him say he looks sad and melancholy. Could he now walk the halls of his beloved hotel, not wanting to stay but unable to leave?

The lions of the Hotel Ponce de Leon still keep watch.

MYSTERIOUS ANIMALS

"Don't think there are no more crocodiles because the water is calm"

— Malayan Proverb

Our pets often become like members of the family. Fascination with animals begins at a young age and grows stronger as we become adults. So strong is the bond between humans and animals that it may extend beyond the grave.

A messenger of an ancient soul.

THE FLUFFY, PUFFY CALICO CAT

Just down St. George Street across from the Trinity Episcopal Church and behind the Lyons Building is a nondescript home that is considered to be one of the most haunted houses in St. Augustine. It is known as the Horruytiner House and a plaque marks it on an outside wall on the street. It was here in 1981 that Pat Patterson had an unusual encounter with a ghost cat. When the Patterson's took possession of this historic home, they never dreamed it would become so active with paranormal episodes, yet in the first week of living there they were convinced.

Mr. Patterson was working in a small office just off the dining room when something passed by the door next to him. It was just a glimpse and then it was gone. A few moments later it was back. A fluffy, patchwork, calico cat. The Patterson's owned cats but this was not one of them. As the cat sauntered off, Mr. Patterson went to retrieve it and much to his surprise could not find it in the house. He looked high and low for the intruder with no luck. Perplexed, he returned to his office only to find the cat staring at him from the top of his desk! He quickly moved towards the cat as it leapt

from the desk to the floor, hoping to pick it up as it reached the carpet, but to his astonishment, the cat dissolved in mid-air, disappearing before his very eyes. Pat Patterson stood for some time looking at the place on the carpet where the cat should have landed. It never did materialize again that day. Over the years, the Calico cat has appeared to dozens of startled visitors in the Horruytiner House. It seems that the cat can never be touched, always running away or disappearing when anyone is close. When developed, photographs reveal nothing.

The Horruytiner House on Saint George Street hosts an unusual feline presence.

If you are lucky enough to receive an invitation to this private home do not be surprised if a charming Calico cat greets you from the stairs, and then suddenly vanishes.

NOW YOU SEE IT NOW YOU DON'T

There is a house that is located near the Old Spanish "coquina" stone quarry pits on Anastasia Island, that receives regular visits from a shadowy cat apparition. From the day he moved into the home, the man who lives there noticed his own cat acting peculiar. The cat's eyes would follow something unseen down the hallway. It would often begin hissing when nothing was there. The first time the man saw the apparition, he was in a chair reading, when he noticed a cat walking up to him, lowering it's head to rub up against his leg. He reached down to pet the cat but was surprised to find no cat near his hand. Quickly looking around the

A shadowy cat apparition frequents this quarry.

house he located his cat asleep in the bedroom far away from his encounter moments before. What had he seen? Was his mind playing tricks? Maybe not… The scene has been repeated several times since the first incident.

HORSE OF A DIFFERENT COLOR

Imagine being alone walking on old city street late at night and you hear a strange sound. The sound of a horse, clip clopping up the road behind you. But when you turn around, nothing is there. In February of 2001, just such a scene was played out on St. George Street in the middle of the night.

Phantom horses gallop through the night.

Carriages are a common sight in the oldest city and have been for centuries. But this time was different. A ghost tour guide had finished touring a group and was walking back to her car at the north end of St. George street when the sound of hooves began. Thinking a carriage had strayed onto the pedestrian only street, she turned to find nothing behind her. Puzzled, she continued walking but the sound of the horse followed her up the street. Each time she turns around, the sound would stop. When she walked the sound of hooves would resume. The unseen horse followed her all the way up St. George Street as she walked faster and faster, wanting to break into a run. Suddenly, as she reached the end of the street the sound unexpectedly stopped. "The guide stared down the street for any sign of movement but saw none. Whatever it was could not be seen or did not want to be seen. The shaken guide ran to her car and raced for home.

Did a ghostly carriage from long ago roll down the street that night taking an old well-worn path? Was a phantom driver looking for just one last passenger for the evening?

40

DOGS ALWAYS COME HOME

Lost dogs have been known to travel great distances to return to their owners and homes. They seem to have a sixth sense about direction and location. It is no surprise that dogs gone from this world often appear to their owners. Is it an overactive imagination or a wish to be reunited?

The J.R. Benet store on the corner of Cuna and St. George Streets is a well known shop in St. Augustine. The owner, for years, has seen the apparitions of two large poodles in her store. They randomly come and go from the store, sometimes resting together at the bottom of the stairs. They are not solid in appearance. The customers don't seem to notice them, and after a time even the shopkeeper gave them little attention when they appeared and disappeared at will.

One day, a woman visitor walked into the store and struck up a conversation about the historic building. She explained that as a young girl she would visit her grandmother who lived there. As they spoke, she described the wonderful memories she had of the place including the two large white poodles her grandmother owned! It seems the dogs had passed away many years ago but their memory lingers on.

Ghost dogs guard the Benet Store on St. George Street.

41

Powerful memories of the dead.

MIRACLES AND UNSOLVED MYSTERIES

"The universe is full of magical things patiently waiting for our wits to grow sharper."

— Eden Phillpots (in *The World within the World* by Barrow)

Since the dawn of time, humans ponder the nature of reality and existence. At times our curious minds reveal more questions than answers. Sometimes the answers are astounding.

The children linger still.

MURDER MYSTERY

Under the beacon of the lighthouse is a small cottage located in the nearby historic neighborhood. An attorney working for millionaire tycoon, Henry Flagler, built it in the late 1880's. The young woman who lived here had some close association with the attorney. He visited her often, which delighted the town gossips. As the woman returned from a long walk on February 20, 1889, she discovered the attorney lying in a pool of his own blood in her front yard. He was shot repeatedly in the back. Little evidence was found to convict anyone, and the crime remains unsolved to this very day. We do know, however, that an unknown woman, traveling alone, checked in at the Hotel Ponce de Leon on the very day the attorney was murdered. She

booked a ferryboat trip to the lighthouse that afternoon and left the following morning, bound by train for New York City. No one could really describe her after the incident. Was she the one that committed this terrible crime? Was there an unknown love triangle that prompted this crime?

The attorney who paid with his life that day is now seen as a ghostly apparition in the yard of this home ... a spirit who may never be at rest until the true killer is revealed,

The dark shadows of the lighthouse hold a secret.

CAUGHT IN THE STORM

In 1850, a cargo ship sailing from Spain to St. Augustine was struck by a powerful storm. The wind-whipped ship rocked back and forth as the waves crashed over her decks. The Captain, fearing that all hands would be lost ordered his crew below decks to locate anything heavy to throw overboard and lighten the load. Barrels, jars and crates went over the side as the crew struggled to survive the storm. In the midst of all this chaos a sailor emerged from the cargo hold cradling a statue in his arms! It was made of the finest pale white porcelain and cloaked in pure silk gowns. The Statue, a three foot figure of the Virgin Mary, was laid upon the deck. The Captain demanded to know where the statue came from since it was not listed on the cargo manifest. The sailor explained that he found it sitting behind a crate, exposed and unprotected, as though it had been there for him to find. The sailors called it a miracle and the Spanish Catholic sailors gathered around the beautiful statue to pray. They asked for a safe passage from the storm. Soon after, the angry storm subsided and left them shaken but grateful. They made a vow on the spot to find a new home on dry land for this statue they called "the Hurricane Lady." Their final destination was St. Augustine, and here, they were true to their word. Today, the statue has a permanent home in the Convent of St. Joseph on south St. George Street. They say the Virgin Mary watches over the town of St. Augustine, protecting it from storms. They point out that since 1850, no storm has destroyed this town. Do you believe in miracles?

All round us... they watch.

A PIRATE ESCAPES HIS DEATH

In 1684, pirates plagued the Florida coast. Spanish treasure ships were particularly vulnerable to the swift attacks of these notorious plunderers. One rogue, the English pirate Andrew Ransom, had great success against the Spanish Fleet near St. Augustine. He was so bold in his plundering that he became careless. His capture came in the area today known as Vilano Beach. His men were sentenced to hard labor building the new "coquina" shell stone defensive fort in town, but Andrew Ransom was to be made an example of. His sentence was "Garroting". This form of execution by strangulation was very different from hanging. The event took place in

the town plaza for all to see. The Governor, clergy, and townspeople of St. Augustine gathered to see this notorious pirate put to death. They watched as a rope was placed around Ransom's neck, pulled around a wooden post, tied off with a stick slipped in the back for twisting the loop tighter and tighter around the pirates neck. The soldiers had wagered that six or seven turns would finish him off and the executioner, after reading the charges, started to slowly twist the rope. Andrew knew the end was near as the coarse, braided rope bit

Swift justice in the plaza.

Does the governor still seek justice?

into his neck but he remained strangely calm. After three turns he began to lose his air. On the fourth turn he began to get dizzy, on the fifth turn the sky above him began to swirl. But on the sixth turn... the rope broke in two! It inexplicably snapped from around his neck. The crowd gasped and Andre fell to the ground unharmed. The priest in attendance shouted to the crowd, *"We have seen a miracle this man is spared!"* and quickly carried Andrew to the sanctuary of the Church. The Governor wanted to finish the execution but the church resisted and protected Andrew Ransom for many years. Finally, Ransom began offering to help the town of St. Augustine in return for his freedom. He assisted the Spanish in the final construction of the Castillo de San Marco defensive fort. During the English Siege of 1702, he interrogated English prisoners for the Spanish troops. What a strange irony that an English pirate would end up helping the very people he preyed upon for so long, But there's more...

The descendants of Andrew Ransom still live in this town over 300 years later. None of them would have walked the face of this earth if it had not been for that one strange day in the year 1684 in the town plaza of St. Augustine. Here, a pirate was saved by a miracle... or maybe just an odd twist of fate!

RAISED FROM THE DEAD

In 1823, Colonel Joseph Smith surveyed his new St. Augustine military assignment. A busy territorial town greeted him as he walked the old dirt streets. He would help this new United States Territory grow, and found himself being invited to social gatherings almost right away. He graciously accepted these invitations to the finest homes in St. Augustine and saw it as the perfect way to meet the towns leading citizens. In one such home, standing by the fireplace, Colonel Smith looked across the room and saw the most beautiful woman imaginable. She was Spanish, with long, black hair and dark flashing eyes. He was not looking to fall in love, but he did. He watched as she laughed and danced, her dress flowing around her. Moving closer, he hoped they could meet and confided this to a man close to him. He requested a proper introduction. The man readily agreed and escorted Colonel Smith over to the beautiful woman. *"Colonel Joseph Smith"* the man began, *"may I please introduce you to my wife…"* The rest of his words faded in Colonel Smith's ears as he realized that he had embarrassed himself like a young boy. The beautiful woman smiled and nodded as Colonel Smith excused himself and ran from the party. He should have been more careful in a new town. He would not make that mistake again. He vowed never again to talk of his love for this married woman, as it would not be proper. But in his daily journal, he wrote of his desire for the love of his life.

Although he could never act upon it, he knew that she was his one true love. Just a few short months later, the beautiful woman died of a high fever. Colonel Smith was devastated but had no one to turn to in his time of grief. At the funeral, he was shocked to see the young woman being lifted high above the crowd. Her family's request to parade her through the streets on the way to the cemetery was being honored. Colonel Smith had one last chance to see her beauty before she was laid to ret. He watched intently as they drew closer to her final resting place, hoping not to reveal his passion for her to anyone…

Then something strange happened. The man on the front left corner of the chair carrying his love, stumbled, almost falling, and the beautiful woman's head flopped to the side. Colonel Smith watched in horror as the thorny branch of an Apopinax tree brushed against her pale white skin digging a deep scratch in her cheek. She began to bleed! *"The dead do not bleed,"* Colonel Smith murmured to himself as wild thoughts raced through his mind. The chair was set on ground near the cemetery gate as he pushed through the crowd yelling, *"Wait! She is not gone."* He demanded that the men stop and the crowd stepped back in horror at his outburst. He kneeled down close to her and before anyone could stop him gently slapped her face. The beautiful woman's eyes fluttered and then opened! He was right. She was alive!

This woman lived for six more years in St. Augustine. Colonel Joseph Smith never revealed his feelings to her. The love of his life went to her grave unaware. His journals continued to express his feelings for many years afterward including a strange suspicion. The Colonel believed that the husband of the beautiful woman was responsible for her death in 1830 when he discovered evidence that the husband grew strange plants and dabbled in "apothecary" practices. Did the husband simply make his wife "appear" to die using secret elixirs? Colonel Joseph Smith believed it was true. Although he had saved his love once, he could not stop her inevitable death.

SEVERED SOUVENIR

In studying history, most folks quickly realize that real life events are much more fascinating than any fictional account. In fact, some stories are so bizarre that they could only happen in real life...

The Seminole Wars in Florida took a mighty toll during the early 1800's. Three times the fighting escalated and three times the losses were great on both sides. During the Second Seminole war in 1837, capture of the great warrior chief, Osceola, came under a white flag of truce offered by the United States. He was briefly taken to the Fort in St. Augustine where he became ill and was treated by local physician, Dr. Frederick Weeden. Osceola was then transferred to Fort Moultrie in South Carolina where he died from malaria. This is where the tale takes a bizarre turn. It seems that Dr. Weedon took the opportunity to further his medical study when he requested to be alone with the remains of Osceola before he was buried, Once alone, the doctor placed his medical bag on the table, removed his sharpest surgical knife and began carefully severing the head from the body of the great chief! Once the task was complete, Dr. Weedon hid the gruesome deed with a ceremonial scarf and carefully concealed the head in his medical bag. The coffin was sealed and lowered into the ground before anyone suspected him.

Upon his return to St. Augustine, Dr. Weedon displayed the head in his office never revealing its source. Only after his death was the truth revealed in his private journals. Many saw the weird jar on his desk and were too polite to inquire about it, choosing instead to look away. It is even rumored that the doctor used the awful jar to discipline his children by setting it on their nightstand and sending them to their rooms for the night. Townspeople often remarked at how well behaved the Weedon

Silent memorial.

children were. Amazingly, he gave the head to his daughter as a wedding gift and she reportedly donated it to a medical school in New York State which mysteriously burned down three years later in 1866. The head presumably vanished in the fire. Why did Dr. Frederick Weedon commit such a bizarre act? We may never know but some speculate that he lost family members in the First Seminole War at the hands of a great warrior chief named Osceola. Could it be revenge?

It is said that the apparition of Osceola still roams looking for his severed head. Perhaps he can never be at peace until he finds it. Although the record is unclear, many believe that the head is gone forever, dooming Osceola's spirit to search for it endlessly.

MOST HAUNTED PLACES IN TOWN

"Education consists in being afraid at the right time"

Lingering souls in the Old Jail.

In a historic town like St. Augustine, Florida, listing the most haunted places is a daunting task. Not only is the town overflowing with paranormal activity but opinions vary widely, Here are some candidates to consider:

THE OLD JAIL:
THE SWEET SMELL OF DESPAIR

The forbidding structure, known today as the Old Jail, was opened in 1891 and served as the St. John's County Jail until 1953. Located at 167 San Marco Avenue it draws countless visitors to explore the life of Sheriff Joe Perry, his family and the prisoners that were housed in the dark jail cells. Don't let the ornate outside of the building fool you. On the inside it was all business. Cold steel bars enclose the interior cells and two-foot thick walls surround you. Convicts found no escape from the twelve hour workdays and never ending nights as clouds of mosquitoes and the sounds of scurrying cockroaches filled the air. It was a place thick with rage and despair as prisoners plotted their revenge.

Hanging was the method of execution used here for all condemned prisoners. There was even a triple hanging in 1912. All the prisoners were forced to watch as a deterrent to future crime. With so much emotion and unfinished business in this place, the odds are good that activity is almost non-stop. Most of the people that work in the Old Jail will admit to a strange experience or two. Paranormal investigation teams confirm that this is a very active site.

Some prisoners can never escape.

As you stand inside the dark, steel cells, you can feel the memories of those long gone. If you immerse yourself in the environment, you will begin to sense movement, hear distant voices and smell coffee and beans.

The 1891 Old Jail is listed on the International and National Register of Haunted Places.

One of the most common is a dark shadow of a tall man that walks around the building. Those that have seen him are convinced that it is a former deputy still on guard. Others feel they have seen prisoners in the cells, heard footsteps and voices in the same area. In 1980, an eleven-year old boy heard voices. He said that the air got "stuffy" and thick. He could not see anyone in the room but heard the voices several times. He quickly left the cell area. Mysterious cold spots and strange smells are commonplace. Most often reported are the sudden unexplained smells of smoke, food, unwashed bodies, toilets and perfume. If you stay long enough, you may even see a fully formed apparition. Some have.

One such person is a waiter named Vince. Vince went about his daily routine maintaining the grounds of the Old Jail, he would often greet visitors as they walked by him. Folks occasionally would ask a question, but most just smiled and moved on to the next interesting spot. Vince just wanted to brighten their day. When the little old lady appeared next to him he was caught by surprise. He had not noticed her approaching as he painted picnic tables out back. Just the same he turned and gave her a *"how are you today?"* with a smile. She said nothing, but smiled back as she moved past him. Vince decided to ask her if she was enjoying her visit but when he turned to speak, the woman had vanished. Shaken he sat down and thought about what had just happened. He began remembering her old-fashioned clothing and peculiar walk, almost like she was gliding over the ground, not walking. The more he thought about it, the less real this woman seemed and Vince decided that he had experienced a ghost. To this day, just in case, he looks very carefully at every visitor passing by him…

SPANISH MILITARY HOSPITAL:
ABANDON ALL HOPE... YE WHO ENTER HERE

On Aviles Street, the reconstructed Spanish Military Hospital is hard to miss. Once you step inside it is hard to forget. During the years 1784-1821, the original hospital staff treated the citizens of St. Augustine the best they could. Although the Spanish had some of the best medical knowledge available at the time, medicine was primitive by modern standards and supplies were short. This led to grisly accounts of rushed surgery, frantic amputations, and unsanitary conditions. The *"Adjustment of Humours"* often took the form of bleeding, leeching and application on the skin of heated glass cups. Surgery was a last resort and herbs were commonly used to treat ailments. The patients often endured painful recoveries, if they recovered at all. Add to these conditions the lack of modern antibiotics

or vaccines and the patient survival rate was dismal at best.

Now in the place that once healed could reside the remnants of pain and suffering.

Deep in the night you can still hear echoing in the hallways the sobbing cries of the sick, the dying and those left behind to mourn them. Many have heard these voices. Visitors have reported being touched, pushed and pulled by unseen hands. Cold spots and hair-raising feelings fill the rooms.

Some that went in, never came out.

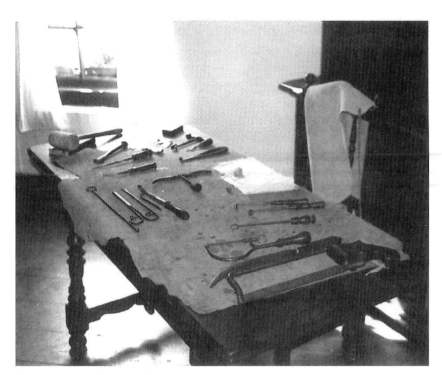

Instruments of anguish

Paranormal investigations document high activity and photographs have revealed startling images, energy ribbons, ectoplasmic clouds, orbs and faces, Objects move when no one is near them and frequently items fall off tables and walls.

Shadows flicker as you explore the historic medical reminders in each room. Saws, scalpels, and bandages take on an eerie glow in the low light. Do these instruments of healing actually absorb some of the life energy from those they touched? Could it still exist in some form in our world? If so, the evidence is clear. The air is thick in this place. So do not be alarmed if you feel a phantom breeze or a hand on your shoulder. The manifestations seem to be merely curious… not furious. They emerge to make their presence known and then slip quickly away.

Strange medicine.

THE OLDEST DRUGSTORE:
POTIONS, PILLS AND POULTICES

Filled with the curatives of days gone by, The Oldest Drugstore, on the corner of Orange and Cordova streets, is a snapshot of the past. Few people realize, as they look at rows upon rows of elixirs, purgatives, and powders, that this site holds a special secret underneath it. An ancient Native American burial ground lies underneath.

The Spanish who settled in Florida converted the native Indians to Christianity and thus required them to abandon their former burial rites and rituals that existed for thousands of years. Slowly, Christian doctrine replaced these ceremonies but some feel that the "old ways" left a lingering impression on the present. Many believe that somehow the spirits of the past are still here to guide and remind us of a time when humans were connected to the earth in a very different way than our modern society. If you listen carefully you can hear the drums beating and feel the fire warm against your face as shadows dance in the darkness around you.

Guests can't help but feel fidgety as they scan the room. During Victorian times, over one hundred years ago, citizens were very much afraid of being buried alive. Unfortunately, this happened in earlier days more often than you might realize. With the lack of medical knowledge to determine life signs some were buried before their time. So a gentleman named George Bateson invented and patented the "Bateson Revival Device" also known as the "Bateson Belfry." It consisted of a bell mounted on the lid of the casket and a cord, which rested in the hand of the dearly departed. Rescuers could then locate their casket by the sound of the ringing bell should they suddenly wake up.

Could being buried alive lead to endless haunting? Do these departed really know they are gone or do they linger in our world searching for a home? Standing in the darkened room surrounded by medical wonders, these questions persist as you close your eyes and hear the faint sound of drums beating.

Dancing shadows and unexplained sightings

TOLOMATO CEMETERY:
SHADOWS IN THE NIGHT

Founded on the site of an ancient Native Indian village, the Tolomato Cemetery hosted Catholic burials until 1884. Known for the quantity of sightings, the Tolomato Cemetery seems to be filled with strange lights, shadows, temperature changes and apparitions. Little is understood about the connection between the grave sites here and the sightings, but many suspect that those buried here are making themselves known to the living.

The image of a young boy is often seen playing near the big oak tree at the front gate. Photographs and videotape have revealed him climbing in the branches above. Who is he? Well, just thirty feet to the left of the gate is a small stone marker with the name "James" on it. The dates confirm that he passed when he was five years old. Is he the one seen near the tree? Children seem to see the child ghost most often and surprised adults can only stand and hope for a glimpse of this restless spirit that hops from branch to branch and runs around the massive oak tree.

Another persistent sighting involves the "ghost bride" apparition. Hundreds of sightings have been recorded of a female figure in a white dress walking back and forth in the cemetery. One of the first reports involved two young boys who ventured into the cemetery one summer evening almost a century ago. They had pitched a tent among the gravestones and bravely tried to sleep when a strange noise outside woke them. Peering out from the safety of their tent, they saw a glowing female entity in a long white dress hovering near them. They could not see her face but clearly saw long gray hair cascading down her back. They rushed from the tent and crossed the grounds in a flash, never once looking behind them. Every adult they knew heard the story over and over as the shaken boys tried to make sense of what they saw that night in the dark. During one such telling, a man they knew from the neighborhood stepped forward and quietly said, "*I know who you saw in the cemetery.*" Everyone grew silent as the man explained how a woman from town had passed away from "heart weakness" the year before just one week before she was to be married. Her family requested she be buried in her wedding dress as a final tribute to her impending marriage. No one spoke for many minutes as the man walked away. It all made sense. The long white dress, the veil covering her face, even the "long, gray hair" which could have been the train to her wedding veil.

The boys stood by their story for the rest of their lives and vowed never to set foot in the graveyard again.

HUGENOT CEMETERY:
WHERE ARE MY TEETH?

Between the City Gates and the Visitor Information Center the Hugenot Cemetery was established in 1821 for victims of a Yellow Fever epidemic. Many sightings take place at this accessible location. Footsteps, voices, shadows and fully formed apparitions can all be experienced here. One of the most vivid recurring stories involves a stone that sits just thirty feet away and slightly to the left of the front entrance gate. Standing almost five feet tall and shaped like a chess piece, it is unmistakable. At the bottom of the stone is the name "Stickney" in bold block letters. It refers to the honorable Judge John B. Stickney, formerly of Lynn, Massachusetts. He arrived in St. Augustine just after the Civil War and quickly became a leading citizen. Just after Halloween night of 1882, Judge Stickney, despite having contracted Dengue fever, traveled to Washington, D.C. for a conference with his fellow judges. Within a week he was dead and his body was shipped back to Florida. An official delegation met his casket at the train station and he was laid to rest in the Huguenot Cemetery with great fanfare. The whole town gathered to mourn his passing. Under the shade of a mighty oak tree the stone sat until 1903 when the children of Judge Stickney, so they could be closer to their father, requested his body be exhumed and shipped to Washington, D.C.

Some were marked, many were lost

It was during the excavation of the body that two men, "under the influence" started a chain of events that would lead to strange consequences. After the coffin was removed from the ground and laid next to the hole, the two men walked up to the casket and stole Judge Stickney's gold teeth! These men were never caught and the embarrassed gravedigger sealed the coffin and sent the body north without any teeth. A few months after the incident, reports began surfacing of a tall dark figure in a top hat and coat lurking in the cemetery at night. This figure would wander around the stone that marked the empty grave of Judge John B. Stickney. Hands behind his back, this specter would appear

Judge John B. Stickney's stone The tree no longer stands behind it.

to look at the ground and walk slowly in circles until unexpectedly disappearing. Many believed that it was the essence, the spirit, the ghost of the judge himself.

Is the honorable John B. Stickney still looking for his teeth or just the men who stole them? The big oak tree near his marker is gone now, but if you happen to wander by on a moonlit night in search of the judge's grave and you see a tall dark figure walking through the graveyard looking at the ground don't be startled… just help him look for his teeth.

Who lurks in the distance?

AFTERTHOUGHTS

When I moved to St. Augustine, I knew right away that it was special. It is a charming town and feels like home. Even when I am by myself I do not feel alone. Although I believe in the supernatural, I haven't really decided what I am encountering yet. After all, what is reality? That's a big question and I'm still gathering evidence. Is it just the things I experience firsthand? That seems too limited when I share stories with so many credible witnesses to paranormal phenomenon. Of course, I have had more than my share of unexplainable events to consider but I also have faith in things that I have not seen myself. Maybe I'm naïve but my hope is that one day we will better understand the things that go bump in the night and they will frighten us less. Until then, I will continue to believe that we are not alone and search for answers whenever I can. Hope you will too...

"When we walk to the edge of all the light we have and take a step into the darkness of the unknown, we must believe that one of two things will happen. There will be something solid for us to stand on or we will be taught to fly."

— Patrick Overton

"Mystery creates wonder and wonder is the basis of man's desire to understand."

— Neil Armstrong

Echoes of the past.

ABOUT THE AUTHOR

John Stavely is the National Director for Historic Entertainment for Historic Tours of America, Inc.® He develops performance programs for HTA museums, attractions, Ghosts & Gravestones℠ tours, and various history and entertainment-based tours including scripting, costuming, props, evaluation, and actor training. A living history "heritage actor" by specialty, he is considered one of the most accomplished first-person historic character performers in the country. His British Colonial period Jesse Fish character is well known and critically acclaimed. His Repertoire includes a 19th century Henry Flagler, an 1800s traveling snake oil salesman named Dr. Dewey Cheetum, and an 18th century pirate, Captain John Kent. John lives in St. Augustine with his wife, Cindy, and daughter Carly. A former Golf Professional and PGA administrator, John Stavely now devotes a full time career to historic entertainment. His lifelong interest in the paranormal has led him to many interesting places and people over the years. He continues to document and share through publication supernatural experiences in historic cities across the country.

Ghosts and Gravestones sm **of St. Augustine**
is a haunted adventure aboard the **Trolley of the Doomed** sm

Join us for dark tales and visit some of the most haunted
buildings in town with your ghost host

For more information please visit
www.historictours.com or call **904-829-3800**

Ghost & Gravestones sm and Frightseeing sm are registered
service marks of Historic Tours of America®.